2

GRAPHIC DESIGN
IN THE COMPUTER AGE
General Editor: André Jute

COLOUR

for professional communicators

André Jute

Batsford

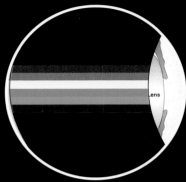

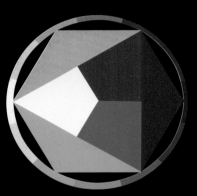

Contents

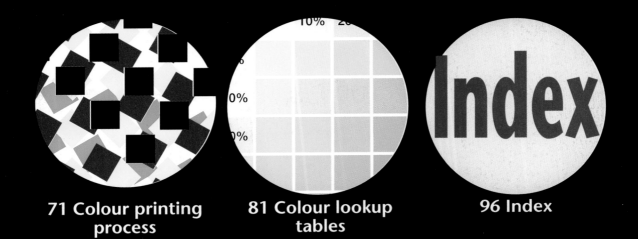

Acknowledgements
All illustrations are by André Jute
exclusively in Letraset Studio, Aldus and Claris software,
except:
pp5-6 in MacDraw Pro © Claris International
p16 from *Tests for Color Bindness* by S. Ishihara
© Kanehara Shuppan Co, Tokyo
p17 in Aldus FreeHand by Thomas Ward
© Aldus Corporation
pp26-29, 31, 72 and 78 photographs
© Rosalind Pain-Hayman
p64 in Aldus FreeHand
by Steve McKinstry/*U.S. News & World Report*
© Aldus Corporation
p65 in Aldus FreeHand by Don Baker
© Aldus Corporation
All text was written in Claris MacWrite and WordPerfect

**A special vote of thanks to Helen Melhuish,
who believed from the beginning**

ISBN 0 7134 7088 7
A CIPcatalogue record for
this book is available from
the British Library

Jacket and interior design by the author
Typeset and originated by
The Bureau, B P Integraphics, Bath
Printed in Singapore
for the publisher
B. T. Batsford Ltd
4 Fitzhardinge Street
London W1H 0AH

Colour is the stuff of emotion, even of religion and magic. Not only our society but every society on earth today has a very large part of its communication driven by colour. While basic literacy is on the increase, the quality of that literacy is falling in even the richest societies. We shall have to communicate with a large part of these societies, if we wish to communicate with them at all, by visual rather than textual means. Colour is the most powerful of all visual tools—and the most dangerous.

That is one of three reasons why colour has become radically more important to graphic designers, the key professionals (with writers) operating at the cutting edge of communication in all media, and specifically at the frontiers of persuasive and information communication, as well as entertainment.

The second reason is simply that best quality colour has become drastically cheaper in the last generation. Colour in real terms now costs less than one tenth as much as in 1960.

The final reason is that the microcomputer has brought colour under the control of the designer at his desk. The computer, in its larger and very expensive manifestations, has been responsible for the substantial fall in the cost of colour. But the microcomputer brought that control and some of those savings to the desk of many designers—and will bring them to the desk of virtually every designer in the immediately foreseeable future.

The net effect of all this has been to make colour the first choice for most design requirements rather than the last-resort solution for only the toughest and most expensive of the designer's problems.

6 Colour is life

Black reflects no colour. It is the colour (in Western societies at least) of death and mourning. Where graphic designers use black, its utility is as a receptacle and contrast for other elements, or alternatively its value is contributed by the shape of the black area. Outside the graphic design field designers of appliances use black to signify 'modern, high-tech' and in clothes black is a 'power' colour. The striking difference in approach may simply be a reaction against the fact that graphic designers have until recently disposed of rather more black than most of them thought fair—and far too little colour.

Psychology and symbolism

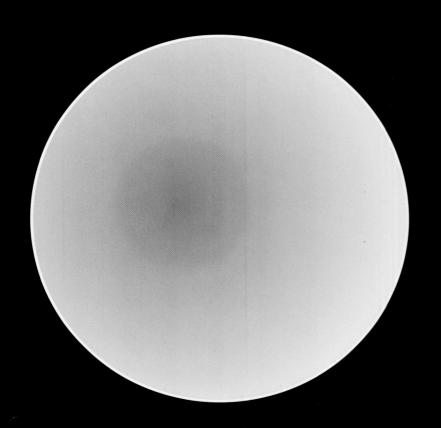

8 Psychology of colour

Psychological attributes of individual colour choices

Max Lüscher's *Colour Test* is merely the most famous of many colour personality tests. Its purpose is to relate colour to personality. It is useful for the graphic designer to know what kind of personality will react favourably to any colour because designed communication is usually aimed at groups of people with something in common. Often the shared factor is either explicitly or implicitly described in psychological terms. It is not suggested that the colours shown are the basis for an exhaustively persuasive palette: without expert knowledge and a complete battery of tests, little can be said about individual personalities. But we may conclude with some certainty that reds appeal to those seeking excitement and brown to those who value security.

GREEN

Firm
Constant
Proud
Self-contained

Resists change
Asserts self-esteem
Seeks recognition

Projects idealised self-image

Seeks longer and more useful life for self and others

RED

Impulsive
Great will to win
Competitive edge

Urge to achievement and success
Seeks excitement

Seeks intense living
Seeks rich experience
Craves action

Keenly productive initiative

BROWN

Sensuous
Agreeable
Sociable

Seeks family security
Seeks company of
own kind
Seeks certainty and
contentment

Requires physical
amenities
Values home
comforts

GREY

Insular
Uninvolved

Conceals true
personality

Tends to stand back
and watch
themselves go
through the motions

Unresponsive to
outside influence

BLUE

Calm
Ethical
Contented
Orderly

Seeks to harmonize
environment
Needs emotional
harmony
Values tradition

Tries to minimize
disturbance
Attempts to ensure
smooth running of
affairs

10 Psychology of colour

YELLOW

Forward-looking
Seeks achievement
and importance
Desires happiness

Seeks change
Values the new, the
developing and the
modern

Restless in pursuit of
ambition

Focused on future

VIOLET

Impulsive vitality
Gentle surrender
Good compromiser

Tries for a mystical
union in which
dreams and desires
can be fulfilled

Seeks to charm and
delight
Wants to fascinate
associates, friends
and family

BLACK

Stubborn
Inflexible

No trouble saying
'No!'

Rejects fate
Dissatisfied with
current conditions

Feels nothing is as it
should be
Likely to revolt

Revolution, upheaval
Fire, courage and zeal
Ferocity and fertility
Love, strength, energy
Evil and disaster
Chinese marriage
Disliked by the
defeated and rejected

Colours carry an infinity of meanings

Luscious flavours and
flowers and fruits
Warmth
Love and happiness
Jupiter
Strength and
endurance
Danger!

Sun, corn (wheat), hair
Wisdom, learning, art
Jealousy and betrayal
Cowardice, prejudice
Persecution
Innovation
Happiness
Hindu marriage

Environmental
soundness
Natural and healthy
Wood (Chinese)
Water (da Vinci)
Envy, jealousy
Balance
Marital fidelity

In our time the multimedium, multi-national communication is the paradigm of the global village. It makes symbolism the most dangerous aspect of colour, especially for packaging and advertising designers.

2 Occidental and Oriental symbolism

Sky and sea, infinity
Coolness, ice
Authority
Spirituality, heaven
Eternity and faith
Loyalty, chastity
Prudence, wisdom
A calming colour

(Violet shades)
Humility, sorrow,
nostalgia
Sensitive and tasteful
(Purple shades)
Wealth, extravagance
Rank and royalty
Costly

Innocence and purity
Moon, joy, glory
Christenings
Light, airiness
Water (Hindu)
Death and mourning
(Orient)
Western marriage

(Plain black)
Death, mourning,
decomposition
Negative, rejection
(Grey shades)
Anonymity
Conformity
Respectability

A Westerner would wear black to a funeral, but his Roman ancestors would have worn white, as do modern Orientals. And the white of a Western marriage ceremony would be inconceivable in a Hindu community, where yellow would be the only acceptable colour. Shades of various hues can make an enormous difference. This is not an exhaustive listing—that would fill a bigger book—but a warning to investigate the symbolism of all colours used as symbols whenever your design will be used outside your own society.

Seeing colour

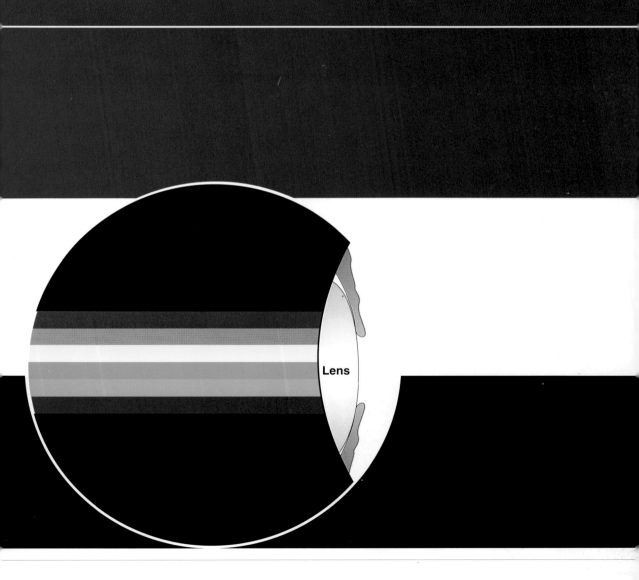

Lens

14 The science of colour

The graphic designer is an applied artist specialising in that part of the electro-magnetic spectrum visible to humans

Graphic designers work with the same phenomena as astronomers and physicists, waves in the electromagnetic spectrum. All three groups are interested in the metaphysical and other by-effects of the waves rather than the intrinsic wave.

Astronomers work with waves from 1mm up to over a kilometre in the radio spectrum. Physicists work with ultra-short waves of fractions of a million millionth of a millimetre to measure the size and movement of sub-atomic energies. (An inch contains 25.4 millimetres.)

Graphic designers work with those waves of the spectrum visible to the human eye which have lengths between 400 and 700 nanometres, with red at the high end and violet at the low end. They use these waves to extract, split out and recombine colours. They use the colours in turn to inform, to convince, and to persuade through their emotive and symbolic value, which is the subject of other sciences like the two we have already met on the preceding pages, psychology (especially in its

The rainbow is light separated by the natural prisms of raindrops.

Richard of York gave battle in vain = Red Orange Yellow Green Blue Indigo Violet

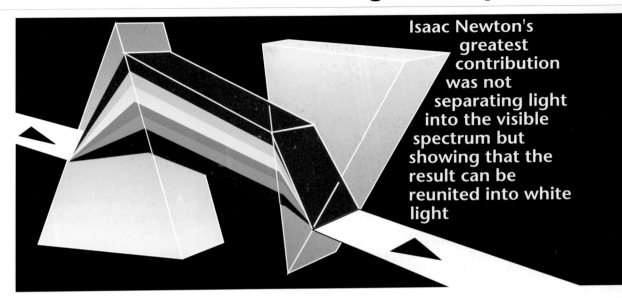

Isaac Newton's greatest contribution was not separating light into the visible spectrum but showing that the result can be reunited into white light

substantial sub-branches, perception and motivation) and anthropology.

It soon becomes clear that the effective graphic designer must operate on a sound multi-disciplinary scientific base—and the most basic of these technical underpinnings is the visible wavelength. From wavelength derives vision and by extension the graphic designer's tangible art of shape, mass and colour, and through them his magic of communication and motivation. Art and commerce proceed from this sound theoretical base.

Newton saw seven colours because he believed in the magical number of 7, but today we don't usually show indigo as a colour separate from violet even if it still features in the college mnemonic opposite.

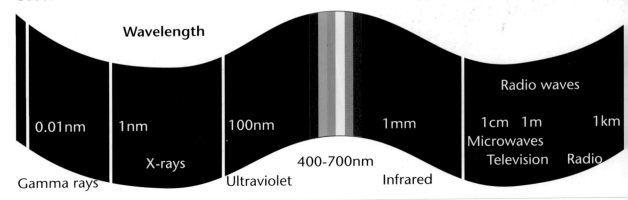

Wavelength

| 0.01nm | 1nm | 100nm | 1mm | 1cm 1m | 1km |

Gamma rays

X-rays

Ultraviolet

400-700nm

Infrared

Radio waves

Microwaves

Television Radio

16 The eye

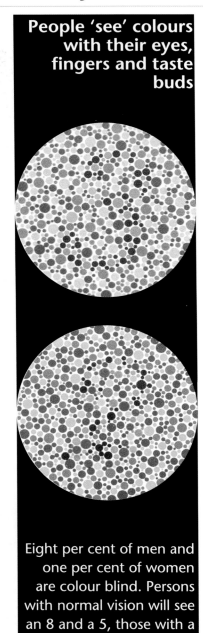
The eye is a camera with a lens to focus rays of light and an iris which opens and closes to control the amount of light admitted. The 'film' in the analogy is the retina, a transparent membrane which contains about 120 million rods and seven million cones.

Rods are sensitive to light but not to colour. Cones are sensitive to red, blue and green. The difference came about in evolution to accommodate our sight to our environment of day and night. In dim light the eye functions mainly with rods, which are widely distributed through the retina with greater concentrations at the edges to give the greatest possible area to capture sparse light. Cones are concentrated at the centre of the retina. In one area, the fovea, there are only cones. Here the focus of the lens is sharpest and colour vision most acute.

Not all light focuses to the same length on the retina. Soft yellow light focuses most naturally on the retina and might be said to be perceived preferentially; it is no accident that humans, given a choice of natural light, prefer a soft golden sunlight, and, given a choice of artificial light, try to match sunlight by selecting a soft golden electric light.

Red light would naturally focus behind the retina but for the action of the lens of the eye, which grows convex to accommodate the natural length of the red wavelength and focus it on the retina. This 'reaching out' for the colour gives red its characteristic of seeming to jump out from the other colours surrounding it.

Blue light would naturally focus in front of the retina and is focussed on it by the lens growing concave. This 'pushing back' of the lens accounts for the way blue seems to recede from any surrounding colours.

The rods and cones are connected by nerve fibres in the retina to the optic nerve which conveys the information to the brain for interpretation. As we have seen, by far the more interesting phenomenon is psychological rather than physical.

However, the graphic designer cannot ignore one physiological side effect. One per cent of women and eight per cent of men are colour blind, defined as being unable to tell the difference between red, green and grey. A larger number suffer from a lesser degree of colour-impaired vision. This has seriously limiting artistic and commercial implications for all professional communicators and especially graphic designers.

The motion of the lens of the eye accounts for colour perspective

Though visual impairment may be removed by an eye operation that, among other things, changes the focal length of the lens, there is no known cure for colour blindness. Designers must take into account that eight per cent of all men and one per cent of all women are colour blind.

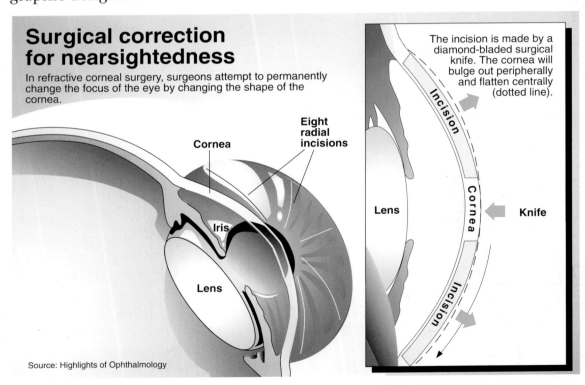

Surgical correction for nearsightedness

In refractive corneal surgery, surgeons attempt to permanently change the focus of the eye by changing the shape of the cornea.

Cornea

Eight radial incisions

Iris

Lens

Source: Highlights of Ophthalmology

The incision is made by a diamond-bladed surgical knife. The cornea will bulge out peripherally and flatten centrally (dotted line).

Incision

Lens

Cornea

Knife

Incision

Colourtalk:
the vocabulary

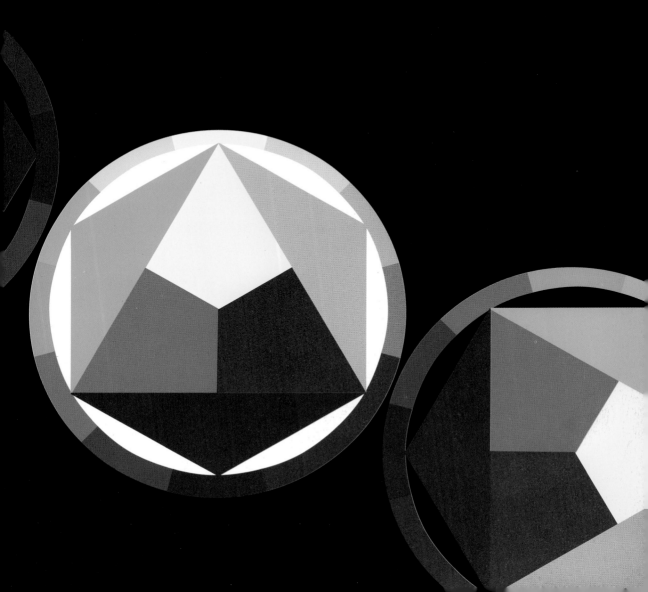

20 Colour models

Which colour? Whose colour? Modern solutions towards a descriptive language for colour start with mixing pigments and paints

From times immemorial colour has been studied by artists, philosophers and scientists. Da Vinci, Goethe and Newton, to name only three, all had widely divergent theories that they defended furiously, in Newton's case with near-mystical fervour.

Today design gurus no longer search for a theory of colour that integrates its physical and psychological qualities. Theories are too soon overtaken by new reproduction methods and novel design solutions to the ever-increasing demands on designers. The pragmatic modern trend is towards compartmentalization and then simplification within those compartments.

Johannes Itten, a onetime leader of the Bauhaus who taught for many years in the United States, has contributed the most basic building block for mixing pigments and paints. His colour wheel, right, now taught in art schools around the world, demonstrates a rational progression and is easily remembered. It shows twelve colours divided into primary, secondary and tertiary colours.

The **primary** colours in this model are yellow, red and blue. They are 'primary' because they cannot be made by mixing any other pigments. The primaries are shown on the inner triangle.

A **secondary** colour is made by mixing two primaries. Yellow and red produces orange. Red and blue produces purple. Blue and yellow produces green. Itten shows the secondary colours in the 'middle ring'.

A **tertiary** colour is made by mixing a primary and a secondary colour. Yellow, a primary, and green, a secondary, when mixed produce a yellow-green. Tertiary colours are shown with the primaries and the secondaries on the outer ring.

There are other famous colour wheels. This one is Albert Munsell's. It is the basis of a colour matching system still in widespread use, which we shall meet again at page 30.

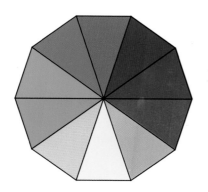

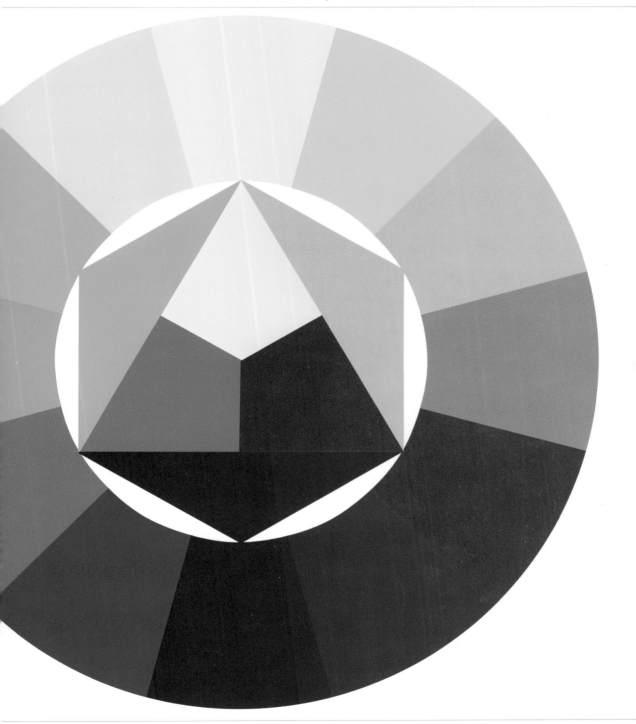

A painter, working with a few colours, can name them. Designers, working with hundreds of colours, need a more practical vocabulary

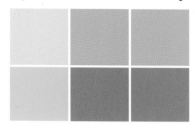

Which of the six colours at left is green? Of course they, and many more besides, are *all* green. It is said that the human eye can distinguish ten million hues! Obviously, many of those hues will be greens. The question then becomes, 'Which green is this green?'

Fortunately, a vocabulary stands for the use of designers, and the scientific and philosophical considerations supporting it are helpful to the wider graphic arts trades in avoiding confusion.

Hue is what in everyday use we call the perception of a colour. Red is a hue, blue is a hue, green is a hue, yellow is a hue, violet is a hue and purple is a hue. A hue is a colour that is different from other hues. A colour model is built up by deciding, either arbitrarily or by some preferred scientific theory, on a number of hues and defining them. The Itten model limits itself to twelve, the popular Munsell model to ten. All other colours are then derived from the basic set.

The **saturation** of a colour describes its strength or purity. Fire-engine red is a highly saturated, brilliant colour. Dull old bricks are weakly saturated. Saturation measures the grey component (equal parts of either cyan-magenta-yellow or red-green-blue) in the colour. Any part of the visible spectrum with zero saturation must

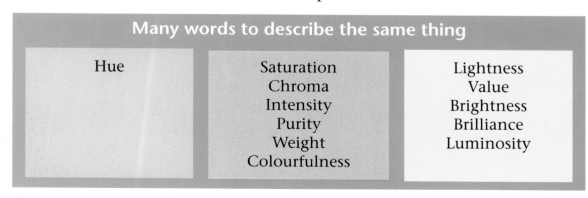

Many words to describe the same thing

Hue	Saturation	Lightness
	Chroma	Value
	Intensity	Brightness
	Purity	Brilliance
	Weight	Luminosity
	Colourfulness	

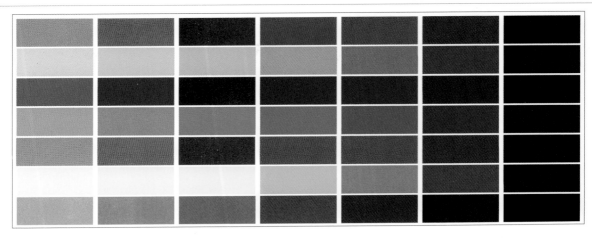

be black or white or a grey.

Lightness (also called value or brightness) designates how bright the colour is. Thus pink is a red of high lightness, and maroon a red of low lightness. Lightness depends on how much white *or* black has been added to a hue to make a lighter or darker tone. Maximum lightness is white, zero lightness black. At 50% lightness, halfway between white and black, any colour appears at its most vibrant.

The **greys** or **neutrals** have no hue and thus no saturation. Absolute black has no hue, no saturation and zero lightness. Absolute white has no hue, no saturation and maximum lightness. A grey has no hue, no saturation and lightness in inverse proportion to its density.

Utility of hue, saturation and lightness

The major use of HSL is in creating palettes, especially when equivalent tonal values are desired so that colours may work together well. Designers can visually select from a swatch book an equal value palette such as those top and right, or generate it through the HSL colour model of most computer graphics applications.

Six colours familiar to designers in steps of 10% from 70% to 10% lightness, plus some greys.

Saturation and lightness relate colours visually, which has practical applications in creating consistent palettes. In each row saturation is highest at left and lowest at right. In each column lightness is greatest at top and lowest at bottom.

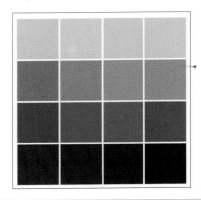

24 Real world colour models

The destination of a graphic design in print or broadcast determines the preferred colour model

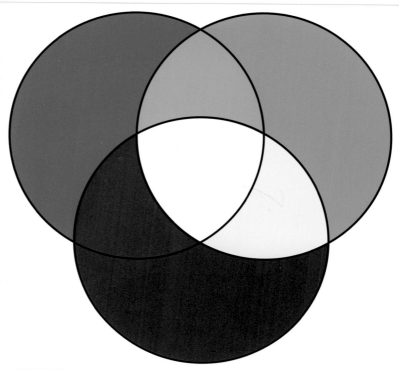

The two most important colour models are the additive red-green-blue or RGB, right, used mainly in television, and the subtractive cyan-magenta-yellow or CMY, opposite below, used mainly in printed work. Their direct relationship—each as the inversion of the other—is easiest to understand by grasping how they complement each other, far right. When light falls on paper, the white parts reflect all light. Cyan ink absorbs red light but reflects blue and green light. Magenta ink absorbs green but reflects red and blue. Yellow ink absorbs blue but reflects red and green. Black ink absorbs all light and reflects no colour.

There are many circumstances under which designers of all kinds work with the painter's primaries of yellow, red and blue. Even graphic designers find use for that model in creating illustrations and in making up visuals suggesting what a printed or broadcast communication will look like.

But if we define a graphic designer specifically as a specialist communicator whose messages are reproduced in number—and most often substantial numbers, the yellow-red-blue model of our fine arts colleagues becomes a near-irrelevance, at best a convenience.

The truth is that the two kinds of light important to a graphic designer are more easily reproduced in two other models. The two crucial kinds of light are transmissive, as through film or onto a cathode ray (television) tube, and reflective, as from the printed page.

The perfect colour model for transmissive light is called **additive** and has as its primaries red, green and blue light: RGB. The additive secondary colours are cyan, made by mixing equal quantities of green and blue; magenta, made by mixing equal quantities of red and blue; and yellow, made by mixing equal quantities of red and green. One hundred percent of each of red, green and blue light creates white. Lesser but equal amounts of red, green and blue light makes shades of grey.

The reflective or **subtractive** model uses cyan, magenta and yellow (CMY) inks as primaries to create a full spectrum. Yellow and cyan makes green; magenta and yellow makes red; cyan and magenta makes blue. All three at full strength makes black and lesser but equal amounts creates shades of grey.

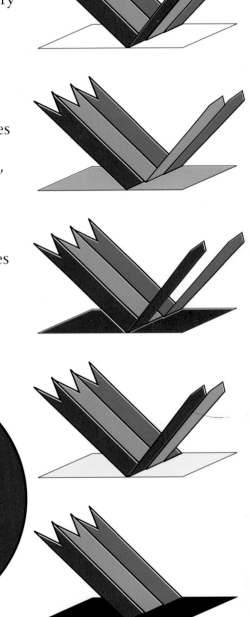

26 Additive colour in action

The television set and the computer monitor operate on the same principle...

The television camera or the computer splits the image into three components, one containing all red elements, one all green elements, and one all blue elements. Transmission can be by broadcast or cable. At the monitor end a decoder sends the three signals to three electron guns which cast beams of electrons onto the screen. The beams may be focused by a shadow

mask, an optional thin sheet of metal with holes which is found in the best equipment.

On the back of the screen are sets of three tiny phosphor dots, one each of red, green and blue. Each set is called a triad. The electron beam focussed on each dot causes it to glow. If there is no beam, the dot seems black. The greater the beam energy, the more brilliantly the dot glows.

All three dots glowing at full strength create a white dot to the viewer's eye. All three dots glowing at an equal but intermediate strength make a shade of grey. Three dots illuminated at various strengths create various hues.

The screen contains hundreds of thousands of triads. Together they trick the eye into seeing the image whole, much like a pointilist painting seen from a distance.

Because of the qualitative difference between television sets and graphics monitors it is essential that those computer-generated designs destined for broadcasting should be viewed on a household television as a final suitability check. The printed images here mimic the quality of the better graphics monitors at a resolution of about 75 triads per inch.

...but the quality is not the same

The image, far left, is split by the television camera or computer into its red, green and blue components. In the monitor three electron guns illuminate triads of red, green blue phosphor dots which, in combination, trick the eye into seeing the image whole, far right, in graduated colour.

28 Subtractive colour in action

In practice cyan, magenta and yellow do not make black

The theory of three-colour printing is fine but in the real world impurities in the printing ink causes cyan, magenta and yellow together at full strength to print not black but a muddy brown. There are two other good reasons for disliking a CMY black. One is expense, the other that it is difficult to impossible to work with paper that is too wet from ink.

Continuous tone image The original image to be reproduced

C Cyan proof. The negative is made by photographing the original image through a red filter.

M Magenta proof. The negative is made by photographing the original image through a green filter.
Right, the progressive proof, with cyan and magenta.

A true black requires four colour printing: cyan, magenta, yellow and black, called CMYK. The K is for Key because B could be confused with blue. The printing separations are made by putting filters of various colours on the camera through which the image to be reproduced is photographed. Positive printing plates are then made from the negatives.

Professional print designers think in four 'colours'—cyan, magenta, yellow and black

Y
Yellow proof. The negative is made by photographing the original image through a blue filter.
Right, the progressive proof, with cyan, magenta and yellow.

K
Black proof. The negative is made by photographing the original image through a modified or combination filter, or through none.
Right, the proof of the entire image, with cyan, magenta, yellow and black printed.

30 Colour matching systems

The key to the largest contracts is repeatability

Because of the visual impenetrability of an actual solid, the Munsell colour space in practical use is normally presented as a colour tree, constructed as a spine with vertical leaves surrounding it. This is a schematic of it. The central vertical axis represents the neutrals or greys with pure white at the north pole and absolute black at the south pole. Around the equator Munsell's ten hues are arranged in sequence with colours of the highest chroma (saturation) furthest from the spine and those with lower chroma in graduated order towards the spine. The higher up the spine the ring of hues falls, the greater the lightness and the higher the value. Conversely the lower down the spine the ring of hues, the greater the darkness and the lower the value.

A colour must be the same at all times and all places. Consistency and repeatability are essential. That is why the successful colour models are indispensible to industry, commerce and government. It is easy to see how a contract to print bank notes could depend on matching the precise colour, but an exact motivating shade to paint walls may be worth millions in additional productivity from its workers to a large corporation.

Albert Munsell's colour matching system, which originally used paint chips on cards, still finds favor with United States government and industry, mainly because it is simple to understand and operate— and it works. The somewhat similar Ostwald system has a certain currency in Europe. But in the reprographic trades, of which graphic design is the creative branch, the important principles subsumed into all operations are derived from the CIE (1931) model. This three-dimensional colour space is mathematically complex but it is fortunately not necessary for designers to understand in detail. It underlies most of the work, such as traditional separations, put out to specialists. Its Yxy conversion is the best model for converting computer graphics from the RGB screen to printable CMYK colours. Industry bodies turn its complexities into digestible rules such as how much ink is permitted on the paper.

Value

None of the multiple complex processes of full colour printing are foolproof. The camera operator can light the original wrong or shoot it out of focus, screening angles can slip in separation (we shall arrive at screening angles towards the back of this book among the less enjoyable technicalities), old or cold chemicals in the developing tank can change the desired relative colour densities, the separations or the plates can stretch or shrink in carelessly temperature-controlled work areas, the paper can do any of several hundred awkward things, impurities in the ink can create colours the designer never intended, varying amounts of ink on the plate can cause colour inconsistencies—and that is only part of a nightmare spectrum of likely disasters, a few of the reasons why only the best designers work successfully in colour.

When the colour on a job is critical—always the case with company logos—it can be printed as a **spot colour** on a separate plate sent through the press on an additional run after being inked with precisely the required colour. In traditional paste-up the elements to be printed in the spot colour are placed by themselves on an acetate overlay. In computer art the program takes care of it. The spot colour ink manufacturer best known to graphic designers is Pantone, whose range also includes metallics outside the CMYK gamut.

← Chroma →

Hue ←

There is only one way consistently to produce a guaranteed colour

If the yellow on this catalogue cover is a critical house colour, the designer could choose to specify it as Pantone 109 and have it printed as a spot colour on a separate plate additional to the cyan, magenta, yellow and black plates shown on the previous spread. The designer and his client may think it well worth the cost of an extra plate and press run to ensure the precise colour they want.

Rosalind's Seed Box

32 Shades, tones and tints

Effective communication in the reprographic trades depends on subtle nuances of meaning

A graphic designer talks about colour to other designers, to clients, to writers—but most importantly to the craftsmen responsible for putting the exact colour the designer has in mind on paper or on screen. Careless talk always costs money in work that has to be redone.

Hue, saturation and lightness are precise terms which may be given a number. Red, green and blue light is understood by those who work in television. Cyan, magenta, yellow and black are known colours which may be specified by those who work in print as percentages (of the total density of each colour) to mix many other colours. Black, white and the greys are neutral.

The problem arises when these boundaries are crossed. On the left is the schematic of a suggested vocabulary for more casual conversations between fellow-professionals than recitations of numbers or percentages.

A **shade** is a mixture of a colour and black. A **tint** is a mixture of a colour and white. A **tone** is a mixture of a colour with *both* black *and* white, that is, with grey. Colour is not always applied at full strength. Since white in print is most often represented by the paper showing through, any colour laid down at less than 100% is by definition a tint. A true 100% of any ink is used so infrequently that we commonly speak loosely of the process of making up the CMYK constituents of a colour for printing as a 'tint build'.

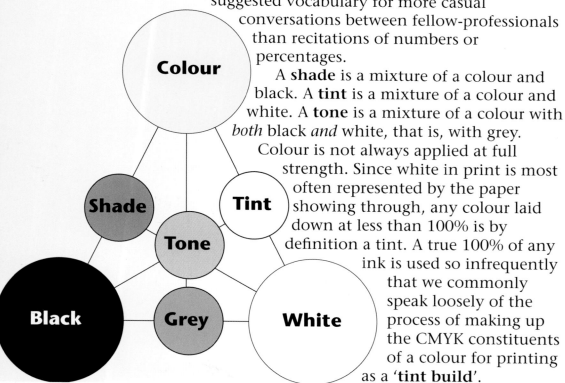

The final item of vocabulary a graphic designer requires before proceeding to the choice of colours is the concept of *variable cover,* which is measured as **density.** Density measures the ability of colours and neutrals to absorb light. Black stops all light and has 100% density. White reflects all light and has zero density. The shades, tones, tints and greys have densities in between.

The density of a specified colour or a neutral is its ability to absorb light.

34 The journeyman's triangle

In selecting colours for a design, the relationship of RGB and CMY highlights the use of complementary colours

The triangle relating the designer's primary colour spaces of CMY and RGB is known to everyone in the design and reprographic trades. It is used in the correction of colour in the separation process prior to printing. But is also useful for specifying and modifying colours in the selection phase of every design project.

The colours on any side of a triangle make up the colour between them on the other triangle. Thus yellow and magenta make up red, and green and blue make up cyan. The colour opposite which does not contribute to making the created colour is called the complementary colour. In the case of red it would be cyan, in the case of cyan it would be red.

The complementary of yellow is blue, and the complementary of magenta is green. Or one could say that the complementary of blue is yellow and the complementary of green is magenta.

When an image should be more intensely coloured the designer may either add more of the constituent parts of the colour, or subtract its complementary. To make and image more red, one can either add more magenta and yellow, or one can subtract any or all of the cyan from the image. Generally speaking it is sound practice to try to achieve the desired colour first by subtracting colour before adding additional colour.

Yellow

Green

There are many good reasons for preferring to subtract colour rather than adding colour in trying to arrive at some colour the designer may have in mind. The chief one is that the greater the number of colours added to the mix, the greater the chance of desaturating or 'greying out' the achieved colour through adding substantial equal parts of each of cyan, magenta and yellow. The most vibrant colours are mixed either with only two primaries or by adding widely divergent percentages if all three have to be used.

A secondary reason for altering colours by subtraction rather than addition of ink is that the designer should limit the amount of ink on the paper. 280% is a generally agreed upper limit for total ink load. When the paper becomes too wet from an excess of ink, it can be difficult to work with and the results are often unsatisfactory because of smearing or ink transfer between pages. The outcome is usually unnecessary expense for work redone or additional drying time.

Complementaries should be subtracted before more primaries are added, otherwise there may be too much ink on the page

36 Hobson's choice

'One colour printing' is the most misleading phrase in a profession littered with jargon

There is no such animal as a designer who works in only one colour. If the designer may or must choose only one ink, it usually has to be black, not least because most graphic design projects include typesetting. But a black-ink design is still in two colours, black and paper colour, with the paper providing the second colour, most often white.

The designer who may choose two inks most often starts with three possibilities for creative expression: paper colour, black ink, and a coloured ink. But none of these possibilities are singular. By printing tints, tones and shades as well as solids and 'blank' spaces, the imaginative designer can create an infinity of impressions. With three inks he can stretch his wings, and with four he can represent real life in two dimensions. If on top of process colour he is permitted spot colours there is almost nothing in nature he cannot represent faithfully or imaginatively, given only that his talent and his tools are up to the job.

But the choice is not totally free. We have already seen that individuals are psychologically predisposed towards some colours, and that tradition in each society attaches a symbolic value to certain colours.

Any colour has to work not only with the paper on which it is printed and the other colours on the paper, but with the surroundings in which it is seen and with the implicit and explicit assumptions of the individual the graphic designer wants to communicate with—plus those of the society in which that individual lives.

In addition, colours have intrinsic relationships to each other which make particular combinations work better than others.

Colour relationships

Colours have their own shapes, sounds and space in the memory of the designer's audience. For the graphic designer who wishes to communicate effectively, it is important to give these relationships equal value with those more easily quantifiable which we shall shortly meet. It is not voodoo but good practice to use to best advantage these colour resonances which we cannot quite explain, even if the practice is more often explicitly admitted in the fine arts than in the repro trades.

Faber Birren, the famed art historian and colour theoretician, noted that when the relationship between colours is 'expressed in line, there is action toward red and quietude toward blue and violet.' This is a concept readily grasped by those designers who have an affinity for jazz.

Not all colour relationships answer to the laws of the 'hard' sciences

40 Kandinsky's audible colours

The musical resonance of colours

Painter Wassily Kandinsky was convinced that colours had musical resonances and many graphic designers who hardly ever work with audiovisual material are in sympathy. Not all designers will express this view as strongly as Kandinsky: 'The sound of colours is so definite that it would be hard to find anyone who would express bright yellow with bass notes, or dark lake with the treble.' The scientific fact is that artists of all descriptions, writers as well as painters and designers, are more likely visually to associate sounds with colour than the population at large. Even more rare, associating *words* with particular colours is an ability found almost exclusively among artists.

All the same, so much graphic design today has to work well not only on paper and packaging materials but also on television, invariably accompanied by music, that designers are forced to consider the musical associations of colour. And for that we as yet have no better guide than Kandinsky's intuition.

'The excitement was a ripple of molten silver down my spine, like a single perfect note played on an alto sax heard over open water on a clear moonlit night.'

Here are some Kandinsky colours and sounds. Red 'is the sound of trumpets, strong, harsh, ringing.' Raspberry red is 'the pure joyous, consecutive sounds of sleigh bells.' Orange Kandinsky compared to the ringing of 'a church bell...the Angelus', calling it 'a strong contralto voice.' And 'keen lemon yellow hurts the eye as does a prolonged and shrill bugle note to the ear.'

He though 'absolute green is represented by the placid middle notes of a violin,' and violet by 'the deep notes of the woodwinds.' And of the blues: 'light blue is like a flute, a darker blue a cello; a still darker blue the marvellous double bass, and the darkest blue of all—an organ.'

Kandinsky and Birren both believed that colours have definitive shapes, Kandinsky isolating the shapes of the red, yellow and blue below and Birren adding the shapes of the orange, green and violet.

They are in eminently respectable company. Aldous Huxley wrote about the mind that 'it evidently feels that colours are more important, better worth attending to, than masses, positions and dimensions.' It follows, since the mind cannot orient itself in amorphousness, that colour will assume its own shapeliness.

'Colour, rather than shape, is more closely related to emotion.'
David Katz

42 Memory colours

There are some colours we all think we know to perfection

Everyone—but everyone!— thinks he or she knows how green or how red is an apple or how blue is the sky. These are the colours we all believe we will know without seeing the real thing. The technical name for these 'memory' colours is **psychological reference colours**.

Scientifically, the belief is a fallacy. Even a single apple contains many different reds not only on its skin but at different times of the day. Every designer knows that an apple displays different reds every time the light changes. Unfortunately graphic designers have failed to convince the general public of this; the fine arts fraternity have had even less success. The vast majority of designers simply use 'memory' colours as a shortcut, much like personality colours or symbolic colours.

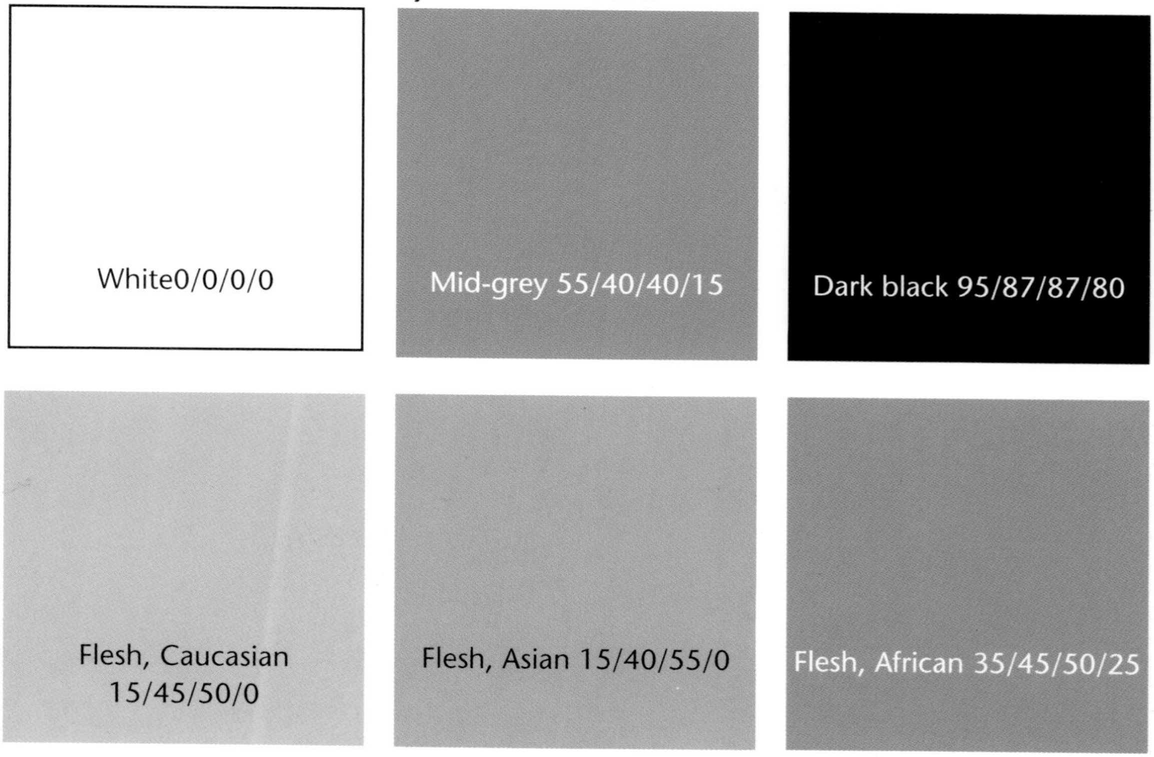

White0/0/0/0

Mid-grey 55/40/40/15

Dark black 95/87/87/80

Flesh, Caucasian 15/45/50/0

Flesh, Asian 15/40/55/0

Flesh, African 35/45/50/25

While the sounds and shapes of colours in most instances make a contribution to a design, the 'memory' colours more often than not act as a restraint on the designer's ingenuity and imagination. People expect to see a particular item in *precisely* the colour they associate with it and are startled when it is any other hue, shade, tone or tint. This accounts for the single opportunity to be creative 'memory' colours offer the designer: to play it against type.

It is likely that more separations are rejected because they do not meet the client's *expectation* of his own 'memory' colours than because they do not match the original. Production departments and repro professionals refer euphemistically to these irrational client preferences as 'special colours'.

'Memory colours' are the bane of the graphic designer's life—but spare a thought for the repro man who got the flesh tones wrong on the President's wife...

On this page and overleaf ar some important 'memory' colours, specified as density percentages in the order cyan, magenta, yellow and key (black). Illustrators add white or black or both to the flesh tones for a range of tints.

Gold 5/15/65/0

Silver 20/15/15/0

Deep purple 85/95/10/20

Deep violet 100/65/10/25

Deep red 25/100/80/20

44 Memories are made of this

A small number of 'memory' colours enjoy fairly general agreement across the design trades

No designer can know what is in the mind of a recipient but the colours on the preceding spread plus this page are generally considered to be a good basis for 'memory' colours for the general population— if not necessarily for particular clients!

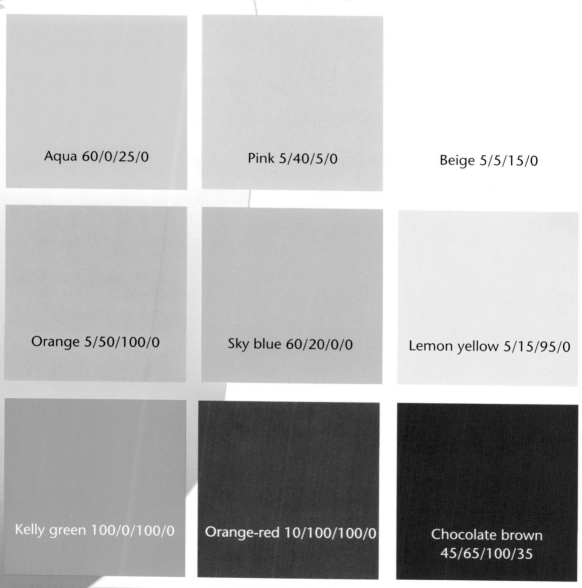

Aqua 60/0/25/0

Pink 5/40/5/0

Beige 5/5/15/0

Orange 5/50/100/0

Sky blue 60/20/0/0

Lemon yellow 5/15/95/0

Kelly green 100/0/100/0

Orange-red 10/100/100/0

Chocolate brown 45/65/100/35

Since no colour is ever seen in isolation, it is the graphic designer's responsibility to choose only those colours which will carry the message most effectively. That may be achieved by colours which work together harmoniously or by a selection of riotous contrasts.

No colour is ever seen in isolation— and its surroundings cannot but influence our perception of it

The red in all these boxes is printed with precisely the same inks, yet appears different against each of the surrounding colours. Note also the apparent difference in size of boxes which when measured with a ruler will prove to be precisely the same size.

46 Contrasts

The designer has complete control over the strength of his contrasts

The strongest contrasts are created by the three pigment primaries, shown in the top three rows with the neutrals white and black.

The next three rows show the secondaries of green, orange and purple contrasted with the primaries and with black and white. These are obviously weaker contrasts.

The lowest three rows show how much less dramatic the contrasts are when the tertiaries are introduced. Nor are the contrasts between tertiaries very strong.

Complementary pairs on any colour wheel are an easy design choice because we already know they work well and provide contrasts for all purposes and seasons. Red-orange and blue-green provide a warm-cold contrast, yellow and violet creates a light-dark contrast, while other combinations provide contrasts in between. Itten and others have identified additional effects of complementaries. Red and green at the same saturation reflect the same brilliance, which may account for the disturbing effect when they are used together in equal-width candy or awning stripes.

Complementaries balance and excite each other

48 Simultaneous contrast

Primaries vibrantly and irresistably suggest their complementaries to the eye and the mind

Each primary tends to evoke from the mind its complementary even in the absence of another colour. Take a large sheet of any primary colour—red, yellow or blue are good— and stare hard at it for at least a minute. Then look away to a white wall and you will see a phantom sheet—but in the complementary colour. The mind, seeking the complementary of a colour, in its absence creates it. Some call this **simultaneous contrast**. A graphic designer does not need a doctorate in psychology to use this powerful built-in suggestion.

Now consider the known propensity of complementary colours when mixed equally to produce a neutral grey. To print and video people a tendency towards neutral grey is not particularly exciting but, when taken with the mind's evocation of the complementary, the two phenomena may be applied to create a supple vibrancy through only one colour combined with tones of grey. Designers seeking subtlety, simplicity, or merely a solution to a budget stretching to only two colours, will welcome it.

In the illustrations the grey inner squares are of the same brilliance as the hues. The grey squares contain no colour, yet seem tinged with the complementary of the surrounding hue.

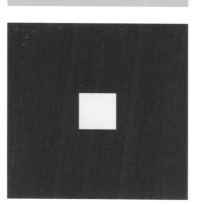

A saturated hue is often contrasted with a less saturated version of itself. A hue may be altered from its base in four ways.

Adding white makes the colour cooler as it becomes paler. Adding black makes the colour darker; adding a large amount of black often alters it drastically. Adding grey moves the colour towards the neutral and sometimes the dull. Finally, the complementary of the colour may be added and subtle gradations towards new hues will result from various amounts added.

There is a trick to using a dull colour with a saturated colour: they must both be of the same hue, differing only in saturation if the designer wishes to avoid extraneous overtones interfering with his desired harmony. Of course the designer may desire precisely that disharmony…

Four ways to dilute a colour and use it to contrast with itself and with grey

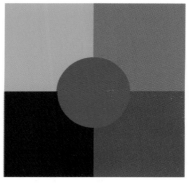

In colour all contrasts are relative

In this column, notice how the red becomes cooler as blue is added or, alternatively, how the blue becomes warmer as red is added. On the right, at the top, a few cool colours among predominantly warm colours; below, predominantly cool colours interspersed with warm colours.

The consideration with light and dark contrasts is invariably one of saturation. To match colours for lightness or darkness, either black or white has to be added, which interferes with the saturation. Yellow and blue are the paradigm of this nettlesome problem.

Matching lightness or darkness interferes with the desired purity of many useful colour combinations

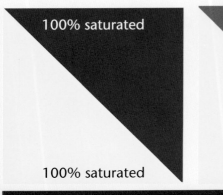

100% saturated

100% saturated

+30% white

100% saturated

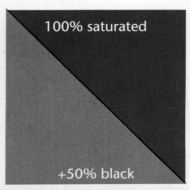

100% saturated

+50% black

Don't make warm colours too dark—or cold colours too light!

52 The dominant colour

There are no uniquely right proportions—the selection depends on the job

Some colours are more powerful than others. If the designer's purpose is harmony, smaller amounts of these colours should be used than of the less dominant colours. Fully saturated red and green are fine in equal proportion but any more than a quarter of fully saturated yellow will overwhelm violet, and any more than a third of fully saturated orange will wipe out blue. Green and blue, and red with purple, find harmony in the ratio two parts to three but purple and blue can live in equal parts. These colours are shown below in harmonious proportions but sometimes harmony may be the last thing desired… That much is every designer's bread and butter, but the really interesting effects happen when a tiny amount of any colour is used on a solid expanse of another colour, as on the left here.

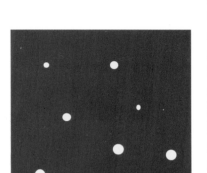

The perspective effect of colours advancing and retreating has a firm phsysiological base in the arrangement of the cones of the eye and the movement of its lens.

The effect is however not pure because the background colour also has a strong influence.These colours advance from these backgrounds: light from black, dark from white, warm from cold, and pure from less pure (if of equal tone). Some colours will always look bigger than others even on the same background.

The built-in perspective of colours may be helpful or may destroy a design unless care is taken

All the small squares are precisely the same size.

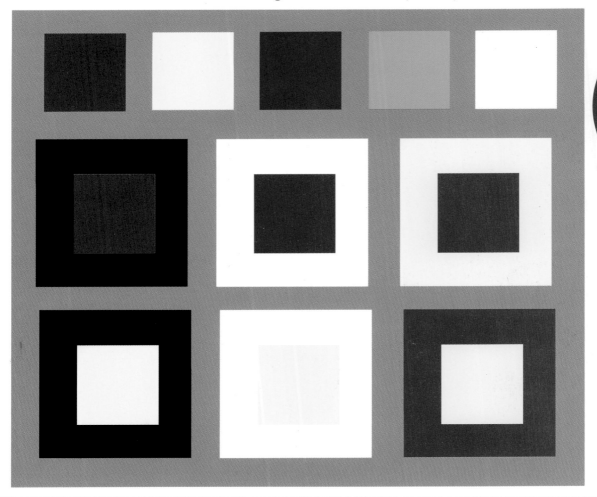

54 Monochrome harmony

There is not one but three colour harmonies, each suited to different purposes

Assuming that the designer does not deliberately wish to choose a startling combination to wake up or outrage an audience, the colour choice will always be for such harmony as is available after restrictions imposed by the intrinsic qualities of colours have been taken into account. The most subtle choice is **monochrome harmony,** in which the designer limits the choice of colours to tones derived from a single hue. A single-hue harmony is by definition cool or warm. Its success depends on the proportions the designer assigns each tone.

Most designers consider monochrome harmonies too close to budget-enforced black and white design to choose them intuitively—or in many cases even willingly! They are happier with the so-called **analogous harmonies**, which find their contrasts in colours lying close on the colour circle. Such harmonies are most often used in closely related sets or families. Their contrasts can be subtle and elegant or warm and striking to order but transitions, while stronger than in monochromes, are never harsh or sharp.

For balance between subtle elegance and a striking message, choose contrasts from next door on the colour wheel

56 Contrast harmony

A quick choice, but not always easy to use effectively

These are the tints from the previous pages, each set with two accent colours from across the colour wheel—but one should be enough!

Paradoxically, the easiest choice for a contrast, looking across the colour wheel, is also the most difficult to keep under control if harmony is the designer's aim. That is why many designers reserve strong complementary colours for areas no greater than accents.

However, **contrast harmony** is so useful as a solution to so many common graphic design problems—in product packaging and print advertising for instance—that every designer simply must learn to use it effectively.

A painter can go into the gallery where his painting is exhibited or into the home of the buyer and arrange the light on his work to his perfect satisfaction. A graphic designer by definition deals in mass communication through mass distribution by printed or broadcast medium. It is a practical impossibility for the graphic designer to control the light on a design in the hands of even a fraction of its recipients.

The graphic design and repro industry views input and output at a controlled 5000 degrees Kelvin, which is taken to be 'standard daylight'. *All other light will change your colours.*

Smart designers therefore try to view proof output in everyday conditions.

The print designer can buy a little peace of mind by working in a room lit by a mixture of tungsten and neon lights and using the controlled ideal lighting available in most good studios only for quality control. The print designer who designs on a computer monitor should insist on inexpensive intermediate printed proofs from, for instance, a colour laser printer, before expensive separations and composite proofs are made. Virtually any printed indication of colour is better than the on-screen version.

Video designers are in an only marginally better position to make instant judgements on the likely output quality of the job 'on the board' because even inexpensive graphics monitors reproduce colours so much better than domestic television sets. The most successful video designers all have domestic television sets right next to their computer monitors and use them to check all stages of their work as it will appear in the hands of the ultimate recipients of their message.

Unless you select your colours in the right light, recipients of your message will not see the right colour

58 Vignetting

Sometimes the designer wants hues to blend, but not when specifying a palette!

Vignetting is the effect of abutting colours which seem to run together and create a new colour. That may be a desirable result or it may cause interference with the impression the designer intends. To avoid the effect, simply fence colours in with white, black or a complementary colour. To avoid the effect when selecting or judging critical colours, use an isolator. To make an isolator, cut a square or a circle out of a piece of thin board and make it white on one side and black on the other. The isolator works on the screen as well as on the swatch book, but for print jobs the swatch book must *always* be used.

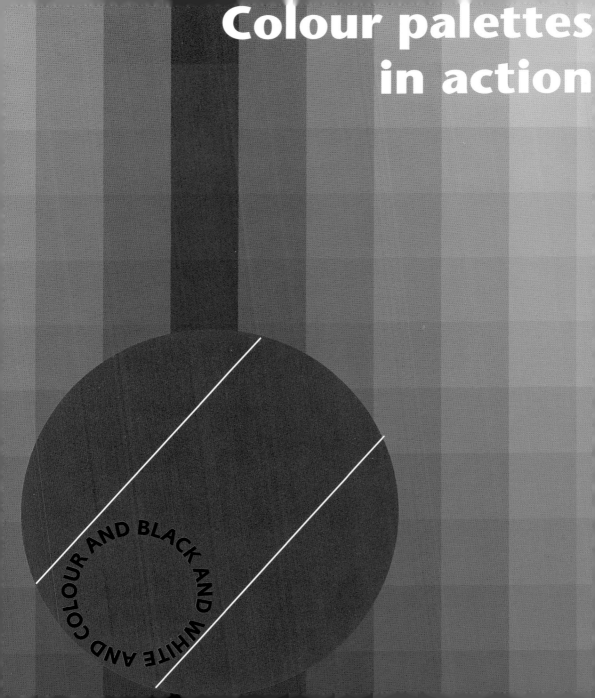

Colour palettes
in action

COLOUR AND BLACK AND WHITE AND COLOUR AND

60 Creating a master palette

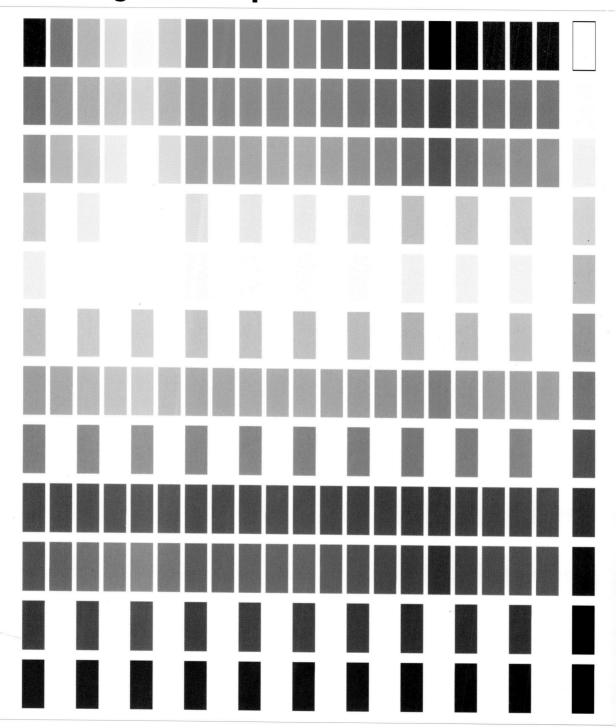

Most designers confirm their master palette when they buy another Pantone marker to replace a used one, and expand their master palette whenever they add a new marker to the set. The colours for each job are then chosen from the designer's master palette. It is however good practice consciously to formalise the master palette to ensure that it covers a complete range. The palette opposite contains 20 different hues, each in 12 equally spaced tones. Tones are colours mixed with grey; most naturally occurring colours are tones. A graduated palette makes it easier for the designer to pick colours which are of the same tone or hue. Reading down the rows are:

Vivid Tones: bright and intense, no added white, grey, or black.
Strong Tones: a small amount of grey added into each colour.
Bright Tones: a small amount of white added into each colour.
Pale Tones: about equal parts white and colour.
Very Pale Tones: white with a small amount of colour.
Light Greyish Tones: light grey with a small amount of colour.
Light Tones: about equal parts light grey and colour.
Greyish Tones: grey with a small amount of colour.
Dull Tones: about equal parts dark grey and colour.
Deep Tones: a small amount of black added into each colour.
Dark Tones: about equal parts black and colour.
Dark Greyish Tones: black with a small amount of colour.

While theoretically designers are open to all colours, most have a 'master palette' from which they choose the colours for every job

The designer working in multimedia, hypermedia and hybrid images, all of which operate at the conjunction of print, film, video and computer technology, should probably specify a master palette on screen. Many computer programs have the ability to import the palette or at least the colour gamut (all the colours used) in an illustration created in another program or in another medium altogether.

62 Is colour the solution for this job?

'Colour is not a toy.'
Jan V. White
'A little, a very little,
thought will suffice.'
John Maynard Keynes

Designers, so long denied necessary colour on grounds of cost, may be forgiven for indulging themselves now that colour is such an easy choice. But there are definitely still occasions when

Jane Smith regrets the passing of her beloved husband **John**

Memorial service 3p.m. in the chapel

Jane Smith regrets the passing of her beloved husband **John**

Memorial service 3p.m. in the chapel

colour would be unsuitable. The black-edged card is perfectly proper but the gold-edged item invites the response, 'Really?' One can also easily imagine circumstances where the use of black and white will win maximum effective communication or persuasion simply by standing out from the profusion of surrounding colour. Persuasion marks the work of the designer who takes the extra thought and thus goes the distance. It is therefore always useful to consider black and white among the design choices.

Given that colour is necessary and appropriate for the job in hand, which set of hues and their associated tones, tints and shades will communicate the message most effectively? For mass communications the colour preference of the majority is known with fair accuracy.

A 'universal order of colour' exists but the professional designer proceeds by exception to it

1. Blue
2. Red
3. Green
4. Purple
5. Yellow
6. Orange

Around puberty the vast majority of people replace a preference for red with one for blue. There is in fact a 'universal order of colour' preference, defined by Hans Eysenck as long ago as 1941 and confirmed in 1977 by Porter's modern study.

These universally popular colours are on the whole only temporarily affected by fashions that come and go. However, they cannot dictate the palette in all situations. Most foods, for instance, when presented in a blue package will sell less well than in a green, yellow or orange package. Even blue has its day, though: a study conducted with the then-unknown blue Smartie used as a statistical control discovered that children loved the blue Smartie above all others!

The right colours persuade the parts that black and white cannot reach

It follows from the definition of graphic design as applied representational art, the handmaiden of communication and persuasion, that the tools of the craft be applied to the intended purpose. Colour is one of the most natural tools for targeting that goal whether it be entertainment, dissemination of information, or persuasion.

We remember colour information longer than black and white. We gather more from colour information about the texture and tangibility—and therefore desirability—of goods than from black and white. We are more deeply affected in our subconscious by colour than by black and white. These are reasons for using colour. Few

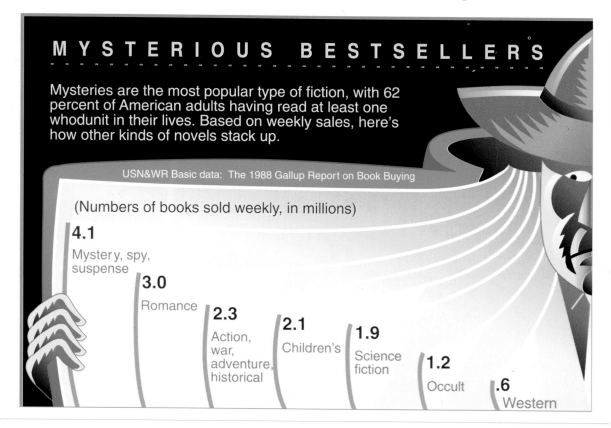

MYSTERIOUS BESTSELLERS

Mysteries are the most popular type of fiction, with 62 percent of American adults having read at least one whodunit in their lives. Based on weekly sales, here's how other kinds of novels stack up.

USN&WR Basic data: The 1988 Gallup Report on Book Buying

(Numbers of books sold weekly, in millions)

4.1 Mystery, spy, suspense

3.0 Romance

2.3 Action, war, adventure, historical

2.1 Children's

1.9 Science fiction

1.2 Occult

.6 Western

Structuring colour to lead the eye

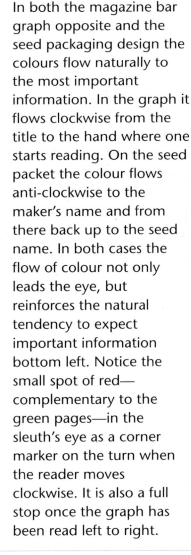

In both the magazine bar graph opposite and the seed packaging design the colours flow naturally to the most important information. In the graph it flows clockwise from the title to the hand where one starts reading. On the seed packet the colour flows anti-clockwise to the maker's name and from there back up to the seed name. In both cases the flow of colour not only leads the eye, but reinforces the natural tendency to expect important information bottom left. Notice the small spot of red—complementary to the green pages—in the sleuth's eye as a corner marker on the turn when the reader moves clockwise. It is also a full stop once the graph has been read left to right.

graphic designers need to be persuaded.

Better still, colour can be structured to achieve the maximum result by leading the eye to important parts of the design in the 'full circle' principle, or by reinforcing the tendency of the eye to find important information at bottom left on any page.

One important application is to use the complementary to the predominant colour to highlight crucial parts of the image.

66 Supermarket shelf appeal

Because certain hues are already assigned particular attributes in the mind of the buying public, the choice for mass market packaging hues is restricted

Few graphic designers would buy any cosmetic packaged in the colours shown but research has proven repeatedly that the housewife knows better. Of the other combinations the yellow for poisonous goods is closest to nature where many venomous animals carry yellow warnings. Green, orange and brown are also related to natural goodness. Blues indicate quality and reliability, red is for strength, and white and the greys 'prove' purity. Designers with pretensions to sophistication find all this basic and boring but it works. Mass market packaging design is well paid precisely because only the most creative designers can be innovative within such constraints.

Synaesthesia is the association of a colour with a sensation experienced through one of the other senses, red with heat and so on. In taste, where colours are associated with flavours, it is a boon to graphic designers. Any graphic designer in the business longer than a year should be able to guess the tastes in the tins below. The yellow is lemon or even acid, the green is salted, the red is sweet, the orange is both sweet and sticky, like a liqueur, and the black and brown is bitter. All this may seem a little like Kandinsky's instruments but has been proven by research.

The colour of food is far more important than the flavour in contributing to the impression it makes

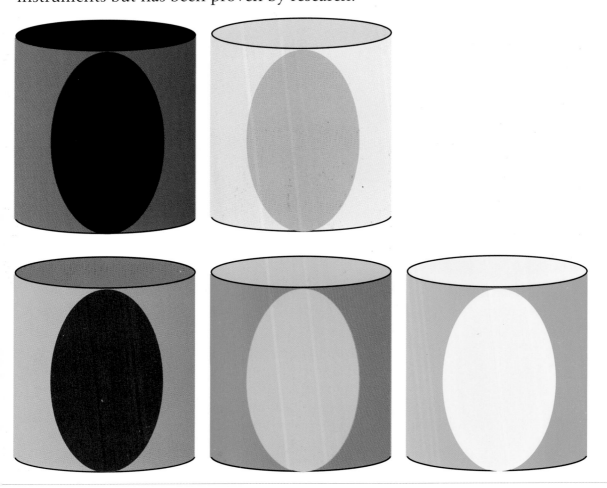

68 Hues of quality and strength

The designer must choose a palette that will not send counterproductive messages

When members of the target audience for the brand were served the same coffee from different coloured pots, they found the coffee from the brown pot too strong, that from the yellow pot to be made from a milder bean, that from the blue pot to be not aromatic enough, and that from the red pot to be rich and satisfying. The same coffee in each pot, remember. Examples can be multiplied; virtually every designer working in mass market goods has a similar story. My own favourite is the detergent in the blue box that was judged too weak to do the cleaning job required, while the same detergent in a yellow box was reported so strong it actually damaged fabrics. When the box was coloured a *combination* of the same hues of yellow and blue, the ratings shot through the roof. Listen to the market researchers!

Early in their careers, many designers despair of routine tinkering with the art of large clients as so much of it is 'corporate image' to which not even the smallest variation is permitted. Of course, if these designers excel at being followers, eventually the best of them become leaders and discover the weighty responsibility of choosing a colour to represent a corporation around the world for many years to come. The critical requirement is usually that it should be a colour everyone can live with for several decades. That is also the major reason so much black has always been, and always will be, used in corporate symbols and logos.

But corporate colours can also be an opportunity. The designer charged with designing a package and advertising for Mama's Sicillian Meatball Sauce will almost reflexively choose red and green as the major components of his palette. They are quintessential pasta colours. It can do the client's product no harm if the green is the slightly bluish green associated with Heinz. The shade of the red, and the detail design, may then be used to give the necessary product differentiation.

Corporate colours are often quality-controlled by being printed as spot colours, that is, an additional print run to the four required for process colour work. This too is an opportunity: the designer can use this extra colour through the publication. But do make certain first that the client does not have a rule restricting the image colour to the symbol or logo. Some otherwise very sophisticated marketers do still have such a rule.

The existing corporate image need not be a strait jacket—especially if it is someone else's corporate colour

Which of these blues is IBM? Answer: None, but who would swear to not thinking 'IBM' when seeing such a collection?

70 Do graphic designers make colours popular?

Yes and no. Today the primary creators of colour trends for all branches of design are textile and clothing designers

Colour consultants are the sucker-fish of haute couture and the piranhas of ready-to-wear. Virtually all of them believe that the colours the consumer sees in the season's *in* clothes are the colours the consumer will want to see in all other goods. Until the mid-1970s clothing led the fashion in colour for other goods by around two years. Since then the cycles for pastels, blacks/neutrals-with-metallics, and environmentals have coincided across products ranging from clothes to cars, from interior design to institutional images, from the once-'white' electrical wares to consumer packaged goods.

It is debatable whether the predictions of the colour consultants that all other design will follow clothing fashion was inspired forecasting or a self-fulfilling prophecy. It has become an axiom of the designer's trade and remains true for the foreseeable future. Graphic designers themselves have helped to create this circumstance. To cite only one example, graphic designers were the motivating force behind the transmigration of denim from clothing to carrier bags to cosmetics packaging. Graphic designers are as much responsible for the denim 'lifestyle' as the Levi Straus company or Calvin Klein.

Graphic designers are not compelled to follow the fashion but those who want to survive must at least know which fashion prevails—and what its shortcomings are.

Various industry bodies make forecasts of fashion colour. In Britain there is the Colour Group of the Chartered Society of Designers and in the United States the Colour Marketing Group of America. But *the* crystal ball, at least for this designer, is the annual textile fair Premiere Vision in Paris, with its Hall of Predictions.

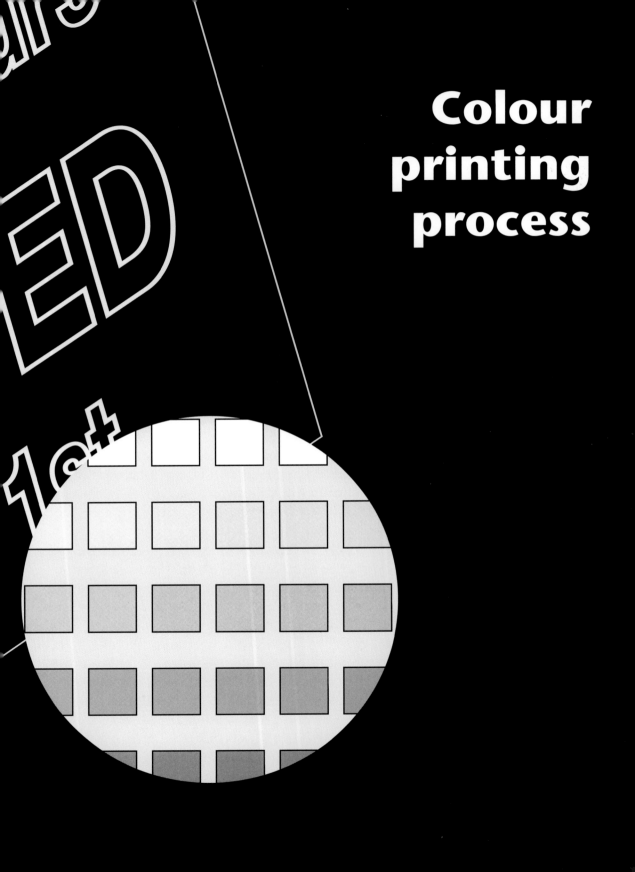

Colour printing process

72 Repro principle, possibility and practice

The graphic designer's responsibility extends to quality control of the finished communication

From the definition of the graphic designer's function as a mass communicator, three conclusions follow.

The art on the drawing board or screen may be finished but the graphic designer's job continues until the message is in a form that speaks to the target audience, which is why it is the graphic designer's responsibility to 'sign off' the job at the printing press after checking that the colour, **registration** (see p76) and imposition (placement of pages on larger sheets prior to folding and cutting) are correct. The designer working in video signs off the job after checking that it transmits correctly by viewing it on the 'field conditions reference monitor', a cheap household television set of the most popular brand which all good broadcast facilities mount next to the 'studio monitor' best quality screens.

Second, because no one can master all the arts of mass communication, the graphic designer is a member of a team of specialists, placed in a chain with product and research people on one side and on the other those reprographic craftsmen whose work is touched on here.

Finally, for reasons of cost, convenience and speed, the output methods generally available have the consequence that 99.9% of all graphic art must be brought to its intended audience by sets of dots which the eye can reconstitute into an image. These dots are now generally called **pixels** which stands for picture elements, because they are the elements that constitute the picture.

A television screen consists of horizontal rows of triads of red, green and blue pixels refreshed (switched on or off) 50 or 60 times a second, depending on where in the world the set stands. Each pixel glows according to how hard the

Pixels on television screens are grouped in triads of red, green and blue.

cathode beam strikes it. The eye in fact sees each triad whole, so the three colours together make a spot of a hue or a grey.

In print the pixels are single dots that relate to the **resolution** of the printing device, usually expressed as so many dots per (linear) inch or dpi. Each dot is on or off, printed or not printed. Gradations of hue and grey is achieved by grouping the dots into **cells** of a regular number of dots. Each cell is perceived by the eye as one spot of colour or grey according to how many pixels are on or off and what colour each pixel in the cell is. This process of arranging the pixels in cells is commonly called **screening** but the technical term **rasterising** is coming back into fashion—just when computers are taking over rasterising from the physical raster screens that used to be placed over art to photograph the dots. Screening causes more trouble than anything else in graphic reproduction, so we shall return to it.

Merely for the sake of completing the picture, it is possible to give the *appearance* of printing a graded hue without a screen, for instance in a medium that runs and blends, as in silk-screen printing. It is also possible to print truly solid single **block colours** by the letterpress method which is as old as wood blocks, technically still no more involved than printing with linocuts, and widely available. Finally, it is possible to print excellent quality **continous tone** images, as on a photograph, without screening by the collotype process. But that is a luxury for designers on lush budgets and elastic time schedules. Collotypes are sometimes used for reproducing paintings and fine art—at 2000 copies per man-machine day.

Serious mass market communication requires lithographic or gravure printing—both use dots.

Almost all graphic art has to be reduced to dots in order to be multiplied

One 9x9 cell, enormously magnified, simplified to show the individual cyan, magenta, yellow and black dots—and the white spaces—which make up the cell. Stand far enough from this illustration, or reduce it to a tiny fraction of its size, and it will appear to be a spot of colour.

Screen frequency is a tradeoff between the number of hues and the smoothness of transition between them

A simulation of the results of increasing the number of pixels per cell or of increasing the number of lines per inch while holding the separation device resolution constant.

The dots are made up along straight lines into the cells we met on the previous page. The frequency of these lines is specified as so many lines per (linear) inch or centimetre. The more lines per inch, in other words the higher the screen frequency, the better the quality of the printing. The process of dividing the colours into dots and the dots into cells is called **separation** because at the same time it separates the colours into their cyan, magenta, yellow and black— CMYK—constituent parts, plus spot colour if any. Because it is a *process*, designers usually say 'process colour' when they mean full colour.

Newspapers are printed 55 to 65 lines per inch, good quality packaging often at 120 lpi, this book at 150lpi, and books of art reproductions often at higher screening frequencies.

Screening at the higher frequencies does however have a price. For the given maximum resolution of any separation device, the bigger the cell is the more gradations of hues it can show— but the bigger the cell is, the fewer lines of cells there can be to the inch. Say the separation device has a maximum resolution of 2400 dots per inch and the designer requires 120 lines to every inch, then the cells will each be 2400/120 or 20 pixels square. At 150lpi the cells will each be 2400/150 or 16 pixels square, resulting in fewer hues being shown per cell. However, at the higher screen rulings, while the total number of hues possible becomes smaller, the gradations between lines of cells become much more subtle because each cell is physically smaller. The designer may specify *both* a higher screen frequency and more dots per cell *only* if a separation device of higher resolution (more dots per inch) is available.

When images are screened into the cyan, magenta, yellow and black components of their colours, each of the CMYK screens are rotated so that the dots do not print on top of each other. The angles normally given to the screens are black 45° because it is the strongest and most visible pigment, magenta 75°, yellow 90° because it is the least visible colour, and cyan 105°. The four dots printed together are called the **rosette**.

Remember, the ideal is that the viewer will never consciously see the dots, only the reconstituted image. Any sight of the dots is therefore a distraction and a failure either on the part of the graphic designer or those who work in the repro chain after the designer—therefore the designer's responsibility. **Moirés** are disturbing patterns in which visible dots appear when the screen angles are even slightly off. Normally that means the plates have to be remade more carefully. Other possible remedies include using less black in those parts of the art where reduction is possible or angling images very slightly differently.

Besides the four CMYK plates, each **spot colour** will also have a separation of its own, so that for process colour plus one spot colour there will be five plates, for process plus two spot colours six plates, with three spots seven plates, and so on.

The correct screen angle for each of cyan, magenta, yellow and black is critical to good printing

76 Trapping

All presses print a little out of register but the designer can apply an ounce of prevention

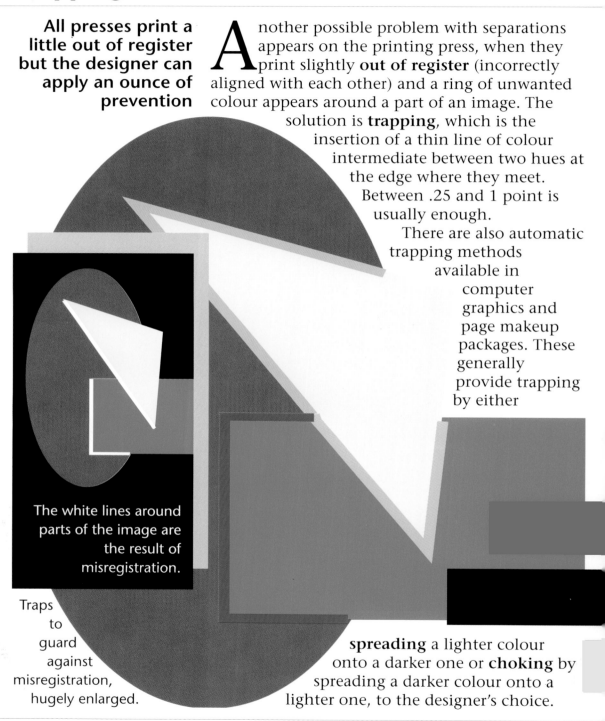

Another possible problem with separations appears on the printing press, when they print slightly **out of register** (incorrectly aligned with each other) and a ring of unwanted colour appears around a part of an image. The solution is **trapping**, which is the insertion of a thin line of colour intermediate between two hues at the edge where they meet. Between .25 and 1 point is usually enough.

There are also automatic trapping methods available in computer graphics and page makeup packages. These generally provide trapping by either

The white lines around parts of the image are the result of misregistration.

Traps to guard against misregistration, hugely enlarged.

spreading a lighter colour onto a darker one or **choking** by spreading a darker colour onto a lighter one, to the designer's choice.

Since cyan, magenta and yellow at full density do not print black but dark brown, a true black is generally also required in process colour work. However, plain black may seem quite dull in comparison to the rich gloss available with the colour inks. When black overprints the other colours, as it often does, the dullness increases sharply. Plain black printed over any colour invariably appears matte.

To avoid this happening, most practicing designers keep on their palette one or more 'rich blacks'. A basic rich black is 100K+30C. A better rich black is 100% black plus 30% of each of cyan, magenta and yellow but printing this over existing graphics will sometimes lead to the ink load on the page exceeding the recommended limit of 280%, in which case the basic rich black comes in handy.

In this book we have foregone rich blacks because there are too many places where small text is reversed out of black. Small text cannot be effectively trapped so a rich black could cause reversed text to appear psychedelic in the presence of any misregistration on the press.

A glossy black is available to any designer who is willing to forego small reversed-out body copy

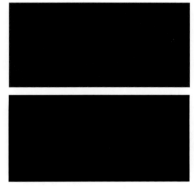

CMY black, top, against standard black. Below, in order downwards, are standard black, black with 30% cyan, and black with 30% each of cyan, magenta and yellow.

78 UCR and GCR

Close liaison with the printer will give the designer better control over the midtones and shadows of images

These are not the acronyms of obscure Balkan republics but processes for replacing expensive, wet, colour inks with cheaper black ink which loads the paper less heavily—and as a bonus prints a crisper image. These are crucial considerations to graphic designers who have big runs of magazines to produce against deadlines, or huge quantities of packaging to fit into a fixed budget.

Undercolour removal or UCR removes equal percentages of cyan, magenta and yellow from areas where full strength (or nearly) black is to be printed. The black would cover those colours anyway, so the result is a quicker-drying print run that uses less of the more expensive coloured inks. In normal use UCR could 'roll off' about 70% from the ink load, for instance bringing an over-the-top total ink load of 350% before application of UCR back to a permissable 280%.

Grey component replacement or GCR does the same for grey areas. Where there are equal amounts of cyan, magenta and yellow, GCR totally removes them and replaces the CMY grey with a black component. It also removes all complementary colours and replaces them with black. A much smoother appearing image results because the black carries the tonal steps and the cyan, magenta and yellow have to create only the saturated, pure colours. More ink is saved.

UCR and GCR are normally contained in the instructions the printer gives to the separator. But the designer should be aware of the process because it causes weak-looking prepress proofs which do not represent the black that will actually come from the press. A press run done with either UCR or GCR or both should look as good as or better than one done without.

Density measures the ability of colours and neutrals to absorb light. Black absorbs all light and has 100% density, white reflects all light and has zero density, and the shades, tones, tints and greys have densities in between. Density is sometimes called 'tone' or 'tonal value' but that causes confusion with those who correctly use the word for the blend of a hue and a neutral. The density of art on paper or a photograph is measured with a reflection densitometer, that of film with a transmission densitometer.

The density of each colour on the material output at each stage of creating a graphic design is the main control exercised on its quality. That is why the densitometer features so largely in the workshops of the very best suppliers to the repro trade.

The most important work done with the densitometer is measuring grey densities. This comes about because each of cyan, magenta, yellow and black will have their own printing plate which will in turn be made from a piece of *black and white* film devoted solely to that colour. It is the making of these black and white films that we call **separation**. It is here that control of density is most critical and where it is most often measured—in grey.

The precise hue and brightness of solid colours are measured with a reflection colourimeter.

Density control stands next to creative ideas, the right colour, and the right typeface as one of the four great pillars of graphic design

Small text and colour make a dangerous combination

The first of the two sample disaster simulations should read: Printing type under about 14pt in colour is not clever because the strokes of any character may be so thin that the smallest registration shift will destroy the readability of the message and therewith its purpose.

The second, reversed out of an enriched black, should read: Nor should untrapped, coloured text be reversed out of any black but straight 100K for fear of registration shift causing unforeseen and unwelcome effects when enriched, glossy blacks are used.

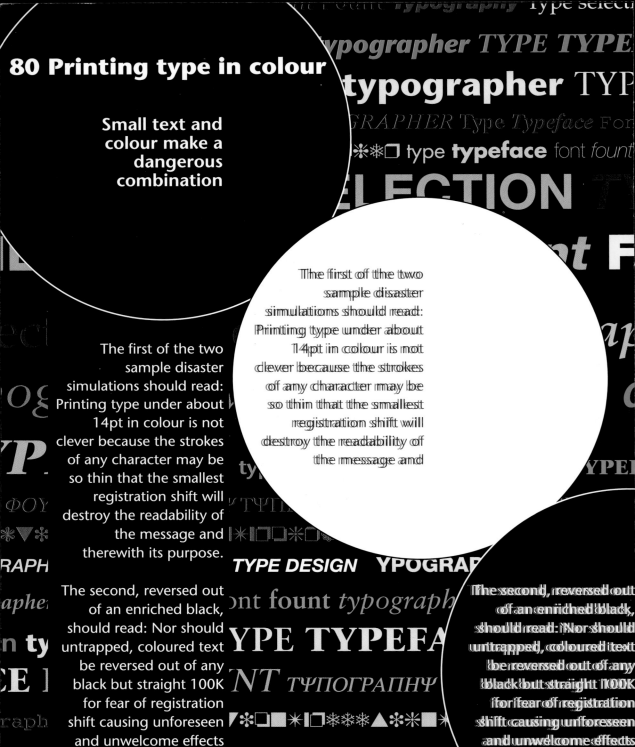

Colour lookup tables

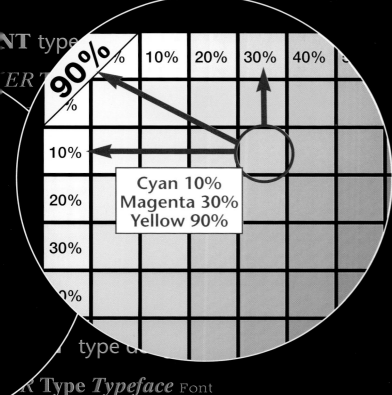

90%	%	10%	20%	30%	40%	5
%						
10%						
20%						
30%						
0%						

Cyan 10%
Magenta 30%
Yellow 90%

Cyan and black

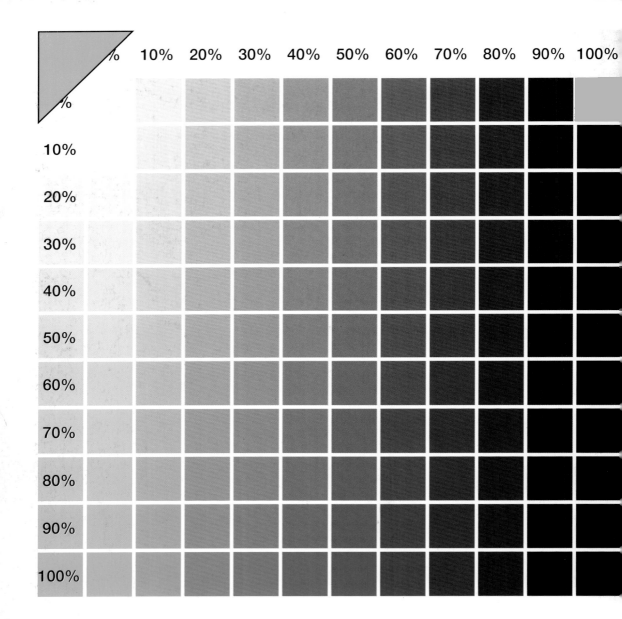

Magenta and black

	10%	20%	30%	40%	50%	60%	70%	80%	90%	100%
10%										
20%										
30%										
40%										
50%										
60%										
70%										
80%										
90%										
100%										

Yellow and black

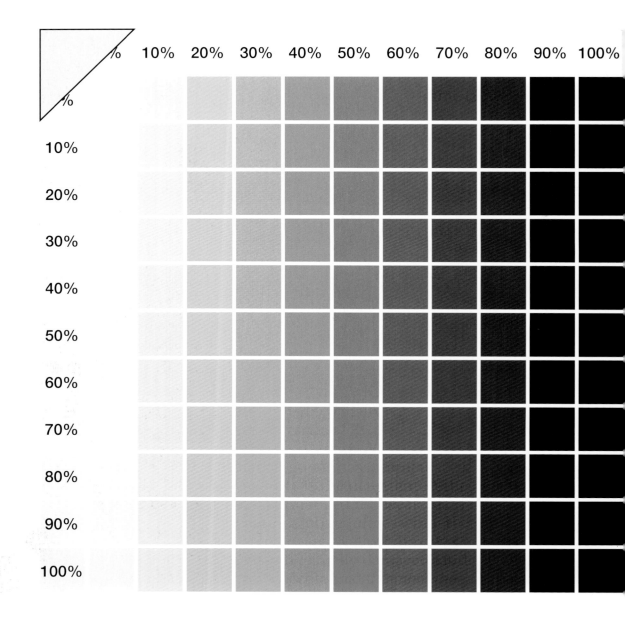

Yellow 0%

	0% / %	10%	20%	30%	40%	50%	60%	70%	80%	90%	100%
/%											
10%											
20%											
30%											
40%											
50%											
60%											
70%											
80%											
90%											
100%											

10% yellow

10%	10%	20%	30%	40%	50%	60%	70%	80%	90%	100%
10%										
20%										
30%										
40%										
50%										
60%										
70%										
80%										
90%										
100%										

Yellow 20%

20% %	10%	20%	30%	40%	50%	60%	70%	80%	90%	100%
%										
10%										
20%										
30%										
40%										
50%										
60%										
70%										
80%										
90%										
100%										

30% yellow

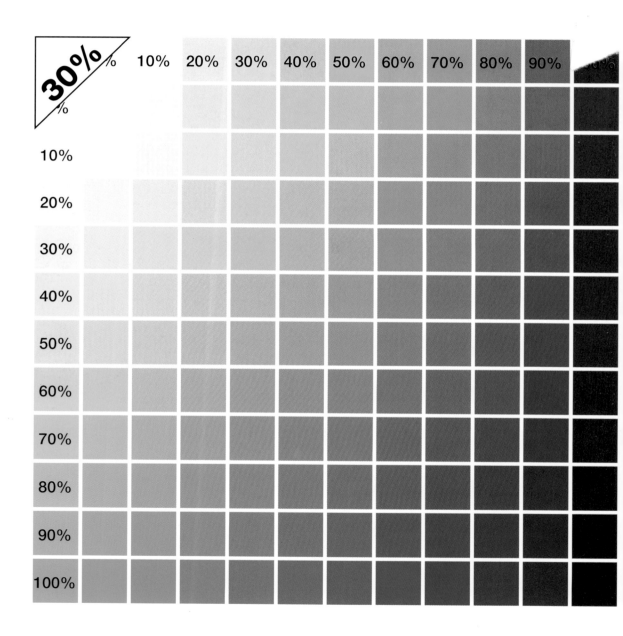

Yellow 40%

40%	%	10%	20%	30%	40%	50%	60%	70%	80%	90%	100%
	%										
10%											
20%											
30%											
40%											
50%											
60%											
70%											
80%											
90%											
100%											

50% yellow

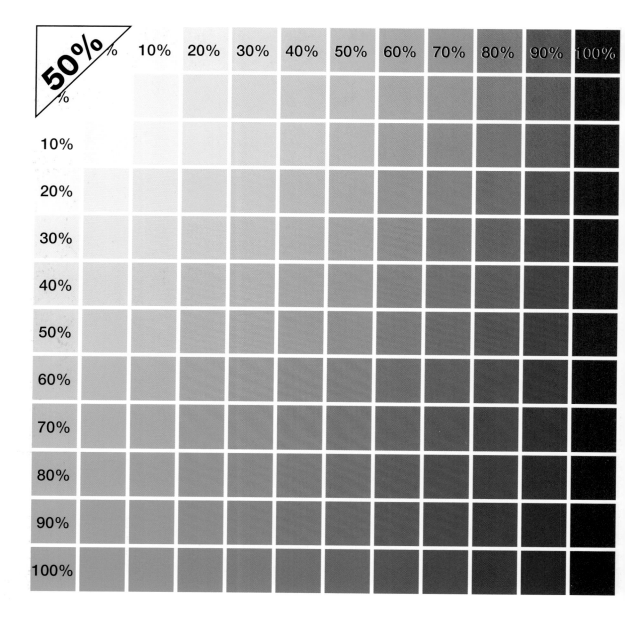

Yellow 60%

60% / %	10%	20%	30%	40%	50%	60%	70%	80%	90%	100%
%										
10%										
20%										
30%										
40%										
50%										
60%										
70%										
80%										
90%										
100%										

70% yellow

70%	%	10%	20%	30%	40%	50%	60%	70%	80%	90%	100%
10%											
20%											
30%											
40%											
50%											
60%											
70%											
80%											
90%											
100%											

Yellow 80%

	10%	20%	30%	40%	50%	60%	70%	80%	90%	100%
10%										
20%										
30%										
40%										
50%										
60%										
70%										
80%										
90%										
100%										

90% yellow

	90%	%	10%	20%	30%	40%	50%	60%	70%	80%	90%	100%
10%												
20%												
30%												
40%												
50%												
60%												
70%												
80%												
90%												
100%												

Yellow 100%

	10%	20%	30%	40%	50%	60%	70%	80%	90%	100%
%										
10%										
20%										
30%										
40%										
50%										
60%										
70%										
80%										
90%										
100%